Anne Collins

My Friends
This Landscape

Acknowledgements

Lines of Vision, *Southern Ocean Review*; Making Tracks, *The Season of Chance*; Albert Road, Moonah, *Seasoned with Honey*; Marion Bay (1) *Seasoned with Honey*; Marion Bay (2) *Famous Reporter*; At Bicheno, *Seasoned with Honey*; Mt Field Shadows, *Poet-Tree*.

This project was assisted in its early stages by a travel grant from Arts Tasmania in 2003 and by accommodation at Cockle Creek that was generously provided by Parks and Wildlife.

My thanks to Kath McLean for her ongoing encouragement and support.

My Friends This Landscape
ISBN 978 1 74027 657 3
Copyright © text Anne Collins 2011
Cover from a photograph by Anne Collins

First published 2011
Reprinted 2018

GINNINDERRA PRESS
PO Box 3461 Port Adelaide 5015
www.ginninderrapress.com.au

Contents

Lines of Vision	7
Making Tracks	18
Albert Road, Moonah	20
Marion Bay (1)	25
Marion Bay (2)	26
At Bicheno	30
Myrtle Shadows and Jigsaw Clouds	33
Kelly's Steps	40
Beneath a Wild Tangle	41
The Hill	50
Leaving Lake St Clair	51
Mount Field Shadows	55
Three Jewels	56
The Mountain	62

Lines of Vision

I nestle into this house owned by Parks at Cockle Creek, it is late afternoon. Sitting on the arm of the chair near the window, my eyes follow the shoreline along the south-eastern corner of Rocky Bay to the sculpture of the Southern Right Whale calf. From here it looks like a kangaroo in mid-hop. Close to shore a small boat with a mast is turning around in the wind. In the foreground a sign on the grassy verge indicates *Private Residence 839*. It refers to the old, low-slung cottage next to it, but this dwelling is not in my line of vision nor in my imagination. Instead I see sign, boat and water.

At the far end of the beach on the other side of the bridge, near the entrance to Cockle Creek, another sign nailed to a jetty instructs *Private Do Not Use*. You can walk onto the rocks that the structure is attached to, but not the jetty itself, left most of the time unused and weathered by the wind and the salt water. This *do not use* exclusivity stands absurdly exposed in such vast, wild space. Meanwhile, the other piece of private property continues its graceful turns back and forth on the water. Campers arrive in the dimming light. At my back a south-westerly gale is on its way.

*

This is the island of wind chorus. Inside I watch dark trees dance to the wind's night tune. I am glad for the warm fire and my pot of soup on the stove. This is a place of testing strength and weakness – can't have a chorus of trees without a wind at your back pushing you along, the wild romance out there full of rain and temper-tantrum squall, full of itself, raging around, owning the place. This is one kind of night, perhaps like the one described by Labillardière and his crew, but unlike them I'm not huddled on the bank of the South Cape Rivulet in the soaking rain.

This is a listening kind of night. A gale stirs up its own dread, reminds you – doesn't it? – of one's ultimate, solitary task. I'd rather be alone here than alone in a city full of people. There's news that another friend is dying. A gale tells you that you're not always in charge. This Cockle Creek place once held me in its grip. I can hold it better in my imagination than out there where the wind conducts the proceedings, where the gale stirs up all that is mostly kept in place.

Living the night. Take your cue from the sound of the wind. Tree shadows lurch. I research memory here near Recherche Bay on the edge of candlelit history. I forget to speak, remember who I am, who you are, beyond all the details that keep us too often on the move. Living the night.

*

Researching memory: I remember the large trees along Planters Beach. So many are now dead. And an old green cottage by the pines instead of the two modern houses now hooked up to satellite dishes. Memory collides with reality, yet our lives are reduced to memory, shaped by it; memory becomes us, fiction flatters fact.

Walking along that stretch sectioned into five beaches, you are now asked to respect the hooded plovers, to leave the shells and seaweed on the sand. Collecting cockles is no longer allowed – it's public property not for the taking. Then from the last beach you enter a woven tunnel of tea-tree on the way to Fisher's Point, its fairy-story path soft and spongy underfoot, leading irresistibly onwards to the whitest of light at the end. Ferns and mosses decorate its edge with splashes of green, while the curved lines of cutting grass bunch in to the side. On a hot day you would linger in the cool here.

I remember we camped at Bolton's Green and strolled along these shores at Rocky Bay, the breeze caressing our salty skins. Our equipment was basic but a summer's day and the stretch of white sand made it easy. My trusting, youthful glee at all this beauty made me carefree. I had a hazy, intense attraction to the natural landscape. I still do. Like Labillardière I am filled with admiration. Perhaps my Celtic ancestry feeds this response to the natural world. But as I was soon to discover, beauty can be terrifying. My first walk to South-East Cape in the mid-1980s turned me in on myself and steered my imagination to the brink of control.

*

By morning the wind has died down and I imagine those campers coming out of a wet, howling night. As the light changes a group of surfers go off with their boards to ride the big southern waves. Fury has taken her rage elsewhere. A spot of sun through the trees pretties the day. Come out, it urges. I emerge to *recherche* past impressions, at the centre of which is a memory of power.

I don't remember going to Fisher's Point before, or being aware of it. On the way there I pass two people walking so effortlessly, they seem to be floating. Our greeting is genuine, three human beings adrift in this openness. I am moved by his unassuming smile, his young face, his long dreadlocks gnarled like the trees behind us. She is more tentative, as we women often are; her mouth smiles, her eyes assess the moment. Tears well up to the rims of my eyes and I view the world through a watery lens, hear the sound of lapping at my feet: the greeting is genuine.

The rocks on the way to Fisher's Point are crawling with fat skinks. My feet disturb their sun-baking and they dart for cover. Another surfer passes me in a hurry to reach the waves around the corner. Focused on the sea, he doesn't want to know I am here. Our eyes do not meet. In the distance his companions bob about in the swell like pieces of kelp. I think of my brother, a surfer in a hurry to get through life, his death no risk, a calculation beyond limits.

At Fisher's Point stand the ruins of an old hotel built by Captain Fisher in the nineteenth century. You can sense the dimensions of this building, the tawny brick-work suggesting an eye for pattern and colour, now offset by the greens and browns of the encroaching grasses and bush. Nature reclaims its own, we are not here forever. Remnants of an old garden feature a cluster of fuchsia and a line of fern that perhaps bordered a pathway. This hotel would have tasted salt, its fires would have warmed and fed the hardened whalers drunk and cursing on the inside, full of masculine noise and brash certainty now lost to silence. The sea and wind have turned the building into a kind of Escher-like structure where notions of space and boundary tease our perceptions.

*

The bridge at the mouth of Cockle Creek separates the National Park from the area where campers bring their dogs, their radios, their trailers, their fishing boats. When the park was up for listing as a World Heritage site, the bridge felt like a line you crossed. Some of the traditional campers who'd long been coming to the Recherche Bay State Recreation Area, saw the conservationists' campaign as selfish. I've never gone boating at Rocky Bay. How many of them have walked to the south coast? A man and a woman stand at the edge of the bridge near their boat, looking down at the fast moving current. We greet each other with friendly hellos – one thing is clear, we all feel happy to be here. Further along the sandy road, I pass a group of men enjoying a beer and arrive at the remains of the old cemetery, now an official historic site.

Cockle Creek Population 3, the sign says. For a brief period it was a community of whalers, timber workers, cattle farmers and coal miners. Before then, for thousands and thousands of years it was home to a people of unknown number.

The European graves tell us 'new world' stories typical of the late nineteenth and early twentieth centuries. Stories of women who bore many children and suffered high infant mortality rates, stories of hard labour in a demanding environment. The remaining graves remember the Motts; William and Ann Adams – Ann and a son disappeared while looking for cattle; Thomas and Alice Field; Rosetta Tedman and Domingo Jose Evorall;* Bridget and William Strong; Jock Hardy.

* I have recently been informed that Domingo Jose Evorall was from Cape Verde, being one of the first from that country to settle in Australia.

Back over the bridge is the story of the Heather family: tough, capable women who ran a timber mill with their father and managed the logs by hand. They built a tramline in nine months with axes, cross-saws, horses and steam. You had to be careful, you had to be alert, they said. A huge, rusted wheel at Bolton's Green reminds us of the mill that closed in 1947. By the late 1930s all the mines had closed. People drifted away. All that European purpose vanished. The cleared land grown back now.

Whales once used Rocky Bay as a calving place during their annual migration from Antarctica. The interpretation panels tell us that the hunting was indiscriminate. The calves were killed first. And in less than a hundred years the great beasts had gone and the industry collapsed. I imagine the rank smell filling the air back then, and the velocity of enterprise or greed that resulted in the whales becoming an endangered species.

*

The important thing about wildness is knowing it's there. At times this seems enough. Knowing it up close is also important, though not always comfortable; often it's intrusive. On my first walk to South East Cape I was alone and in the bright February light, nature exposed my sense of solitude to its core: a savage, intimate aloneness beneath an intense blue sky, the sun's shadows sharp and unrelenting. That walk threw me into myself and out of control.

I have been on this same walk with others a few times since. Parks and Wildlife call it a great short walk and it is. Yet I became so afraid that first time. Was it simply the snakes? I think not, although they played havoc with my mind. I can be rational about snakes when I only see one every now and then. But there was more to it than this feeling of deep discomfort: that day out there I did not linger.

Now all these years later, it's a still April morning and I venture into a cathedral of trees resonant with birdsong. Honeyeaters and pale brown finches scatter on my approach. This is a morning sitting softly between overcast and sunny. I pause before descending into Blowhole Valley, a wide carpet-like tapestry of brown, pink and grey grasses with a scattering of heath-like shrubs and trees. Old fence posts nearly smothered by vegetation, slant in a line across ways. I try to imagine a tram going through here or someone trying to raise cattle in this country. Easy to imagine losing them. Today a neat wooden walking track stretches ahead of the walker, a kind of 'yellow brick road' you can skip along, enticing, easy to follow.

On a calm autumn morning like this, Blowhole Valley gives you a benign welcome. You can hear the ocean roar beyond the hills at the other end.

You the silent walker with the light changing ever so slightly from second to second. Second by second the shadows move, second by second you feel a kind of love. Second by second is as close as you'll get in this life, to time standing still. And yet, just the other night, you know this place was being blasted.

*

What was I afraid of that February day I went on my first walk through this valley? I'd already experienced the 'wilderness' and felt drawn to it. I had expectations of being filled with the radiance that a sparkling, hot Tasmanian day can bring. Determined to go, I rushed towards this possibility, then very soon found myself trapped by fear in too-bright light. By the time I reached the ocean I could barely look at it, its roar seemed menacing. I crouched behind bushes feeling like I'd never get back to the gentle waters at Rocky Bay. I certainly don't remember sitting on the expansive black cliff at the eastern end of the beach with its full-of-wonder view. Maybe I'd had too much sun. Maybe my mind was on fire.

The short walk that day seemed endless and all consuming, as if the sea would swallow me up, or I would disappear like the long-ago Ann. Perhaps she was whispering sweet dread into my ears, although I didn't know about her then. I stayed huddled at the coast only for as long as it took to eat my sandwich, then faced the task of getting back. It felt like a six-kilometre test of will and bravery. This sounds so ridiculous now and yet it was dramatic. My head felt like it would burst as wave after wave of anxiety came over me. Being threatened by wildness was a great shock to me because I'd prided myself on feeling one with it. But that day Mother Nature was the hard taskmistress.

Without the ease of cleared wooden walkways, the old path was narrow, muddy and on that day literally oozing – four big tiger snakes in the space of ten minutes made it seem like they were there every inch of the way from then on. Every stick, every tree root, every passage lined with tall cutting grass was, in my mind, a snake place. The idea of snakes took over and so they were everywhere. I don't remember actually seeing any more big snakes after that, but I expected to every minute of the way which was worse.

The tiny bit of my rational mind that was still working that afternoon tried to say: the beauty, the beauty, what about the beauty? Well, it was there, in all its cruel magnificence, it seemed.

When I reached the other end of the valley again, just before heading back up to the eucalypt forest, I glanced down at my feet and saw that I'd almost trodden on a whip snake. It spun a sudden circle or two as if to have the last laugh, before slithering just as quickly out of sight. The final unnerving. Alice was certainly in Wonderland but it was merciless that afternoon. Or was the little green whip snake Oz the Great and Terrible? I was by then overwrought with fear as I charged off through the trees lest I stop and become immobilised. The track narrowed through more cutting grass, I slipped, the grasses cut my hands. I forged on, beside myself.

*

This time the full roar of the Great Southern Ocean greets me like a gentle sleep-breathing giant and from up top the water is a heaving mass of black, laced with gushing white. People on the beach are minuscule. Seabird sounds are minuscule. I feel gloriously minuscule.

Down below, lying on the sand the roar comes inside you, you become the roar. It vibrates over the ground, across your back, it closes in on you. You are sound, the roar is you. You want to be lost in the roar. Words lose their shape, thinking loses its shape, sleep loses its shape. The giant breathes and you know its froth could toss you aside forever, in less than a moment it could be all over.

The sun soothes. A woman, who looks like a tiny patch of sparkling red from here, stands on one of the many chocolate brown boulders strewn across the western end of the beach. As the heavy waves bang up against these rocks, spray erupts high into the air above her.

After some time, the sea mist rolls in, ethereal, beckoning. When I leave, I leave haltingly as if I am leaving a lover. I turn back again and again.

Then out of left field a man walks by, all too neatly dressed in new gear, like a scene from a Merchant Ivory film. He's a pale foreign hunter in the antipodes, carrying a tripod like a gun, striding towards the wooden stairway at the end of the beach. It will lead him to heaven and maybe a bit of hell on the South Coast track. He's off to capture those moments savoured later when he will look at his photos and remember. But he's the one who'll be captured. I imagine the exertion and the exhilaration.

*

Away from the water, back through the tea-tree groves all you hear is bird twitter and leaf tinkle. A carpet of composted foliage welcomes you underfoot, as you wander past stands of native laurel, treeferns, trickle-creek sounds, rock pools swirling with foam patterns beneath the bracken laden banks in the dappled light. After that the sandy path continues, criss-crossing with snake-sticks, meandering further from the coast than you might expect, a lasting reminder of the beach.

I come upon a group of feeding black cockatoos, one drops a banksia cone in front of me as they object piercingly to my presence, screeching on and on for ages – okay, I say, I'm going.

Memory being at least half-fiction, what you see, what you hear the next time is never the same. I'd always remembered dark mountain ridges looming over the valley, but there are none. The spectacular chain known as The Cockscomb, Mount Leillateah and Moonlight Ridge are not actually visible from the valley, I realise. To see them, you have to get to the other side of the eucalypts near the beginning of the track. When I arrived back at our camp spot all those years ago, I dived into the glassy water at Rocky Bay and washed away my fears. As I picture it, there were fairy penguins playing in the water. Fact or fiction? Since those days I've known whole 'remembered' hillsides not to be there when I've gone back to find them, lost in the weave of story, invisible yet wholly present.

*

The vibrant pink of the robin, the dark purple of the climbing blueberry, the seaweed patterns on the sand, kelp glistening in a bubbling sea, feasting cockatoos – some of us feel nurtured by these encounters. Some people come for the big adventure, park their cars in the long-term parking area, wrap their legs with gaiters ready for the mud, their packs loaded for all kinds of weather, all kinds of life and possibly near-death experiences. Still others might come here and think there was nothing much to do. They would welcome a visitors' centre, somewhere inside to go to, eighty comfortable cabins to stay in, a bar and restaurant. Some people who pull up here, don't even get out of their cars. For a while along the road through Bolton's Green, surveyors' pegs stood ready marking a plan.

This is the land of the Lylue-quonny bands of the South West tribe. Their places: Needwonee known now as Cox's Bight; Ninene renamed Port Davey; Lowreene – Low Rocky Point. There have long been people here. Yet one of the myths of my generation is the myth of 'wilderness' as in uninhabited, untouched, pristine. I can no longer see the Tasmanian landscape in these terms, though I used to, with an awe and reverence that was, nevertheless, ahistorical and Eurocentric. Perhaps 'wilderness' as in 'pristine' is meaningful in a relative sense – relative say, to what you would find in Europe. I've never gone far enough into so-called 'deep wilderness' to really know if it exists. The 'wilderness' photography of the past fifty years helps us appreciate the breathtaking, uncultivated landscape that does exist here and why it's worth preserving. But the notion of 'untouched' country seems to me to be a non-indigenous fantasy. Many 'discoverers' of so-called 'wilderness' have done so in the company of indigenous people or after the fact, people whose pivotal role in the landscape is unknown, ignored or relegated to the margins of an overblown explorer narrative.

Even though history re-tells us that this place was full of human life and culture well before Europeans got here, the contemporary craving for 'pristine wilderness' experience is on the increase. And this desire is placing the environment under a new kind of stress, thereby changing it again.

Outside the door of the cottage I am confronted by two enormous clouds of smoke billowing upwards from behind the hills at the northern end of the bay. As the smoke rises up, its dense centres red-brown like spent blood, merge into mushroom-stalk brown and flower into a white-grey curling mass. There is a kind of grandeur to it all. But these are Forestry's regeneration burns and every autumn people argue fiercely about them.

The smoke drifts east, then out to sea, forming a murky umbrella over the southern tip of Bruny Island. I fix my gaze west on the silhouette of mountain ridges beneath a sky of blended reds, browns, purples, greys and yellows – a painter's delight.

If the indigenous custodians of this land had been left to continue their traditions, we would have another story of fire. We are learning that they patterned the landscape with fire, transforming it in sustainable cycles in accordance with indigenous law. As Bill Gammage reminds us, 'When you go into the bush, or into what Europeans call wilderness, the memory, monuments and memorials of the Tasmanians will be all around you.'

*

The currawongs are having a party in the rain. On a grey day all colour is intensified. Cloud grey, quiet grey, lazy lapping water grey, slow grey, lines of light grey across liquid flat. A man stands in the rain beside his mobile home, like a tortoise out of his shell. Three plovers on the beach give me wide berth, circle over the water to land behind me. A speck of a boat in the middle of the bay carries the secrets of two paddlers across the water's surface as they share a joke, one scoffs a knowing laugh. Grey does not hurry. Even a sudden windy whip of dark grey moving low across the bay and dumping rain, means you crouch down by the acacia bushes, watch the performance, watch the paddlers work their sticks back towards the shore, only to slow down again once the cranky cloud has moved on. I am the calm fabric of grey.

I feel like I am being absorbed into this landscape. I want to be like a rock with a lusty shine, all sea salty, ageing grain by grain. Now a cacophony of parrots is celebrating the day. Do we really need an hotel here? At least the developers have, of late, agreed to build their tourist facility outside the National Park zone.

The afternoon light settles on a small circular island of rocks not far from the shore, a necklace of gulls crowd around its edge for a snooze. A quiescent moment, full of life.

References
1. Edward Duyker, *Citizen Labillardière*, MUP, 2003.
2. 'Landscapes Transformed' by Bill Gammage, page 165 in *Memory, Monuments and Museums*, Marilyn Lake (ed.), MUP, 2006.

Making Tracks

I

She-oak shimmer, she-oak whisper shshsh…
your secrets in the breeze.
Wallabies chewing in your shade,
their gaze fixed on the haze beyond.
Castles of granite stand steadfast at your back,
along the path mauve orchids, tiny at your feet,
and the dancing parrot-pea, so yellow, so look-at-me.
The perfume of honey wafts and whiffs.
Picture all this, and across the bay a
sheen of grey as the afternoon lowers its light.

II

I went back the way I came but going back
is never the same, never just the reverse,
a mirror opposite of what you saw before,
the idea of nothing new, or even déjà-vu.
You stood on the rock, line down to the sea,
and pulled an ugly fish from the sparkle.
It's just a cod, you said, unimpressed.
Did you throw it back? Or did we eat it
in that shabby shack, its lino peeled and pressed
by years of holiday dirt pinched into place.
In my dreams your fish glistened and
under the luck of stars we brought its taste to life,
spoke of all those unmentionable things like love.
But it wasn't so – with me too awkward and
you just *helpless, helpless, helpless*, as you used to sing.

III

The tracks have changed, I have changed and
yet this place can seem as untamed as ever. Still,
you're the spirit amongst us now, caught up
in the mystery we all hanker for; we've still so
much to learn. As if footprints aren't enough,
the litter on the forest floor attests,
the ultimate disrespect of butt and tissue,
it's time we stayed away from here, where
the smell of east-coast rock lingers, sun, sand, salt.
These hazards take their toll. Across the liquid quiet
the green house stands emptied of its dream. And
in the dying light those mountains soften to pink
as the last toc of the tennis ball is heard coming
from the lodge. Now everything is still and readying
for the night, readying for more than the end of a day.

Note: this poem was inspired by times spent at Coles Bay.

Albert Road, Moonah

1

In 1978 we rented a house, its life about to end.
Zoned commercial the sign for sale ignored its forties charm,
its solid weatherboard, the veranda cornering the sun
where a few stray hollyhocks beamed like showgirls.
Suburban grace about to be displaced.
Our furniture sparse and second-hand –
table, chairs, mattresses on the floor, and cushions
propped against the floral wallpaper,
a dizzy forest of white, yellow and green,
filled the space from ceiling to carpet,
swirling grey and red roses.

2

A concrete path out the back cracked its way to the laundry shed,
then raspberries and gooseberries stretched to the fence –
we knew nothing of pruning or tending. In Sydney they came in a tin.
But at Albert Road we laughed going out the door to pick breakfast
an exotic bowl of fruit, tart and topped with cream.

3

At Albert Road I bought a piano.
Each morning I gazed up from the floor at its stately chest,
and in the afternoon played a beginner's Tchaikovsky and Chopin.
The sun streamed through the window facing west
onto hills and mountains alive in pure cold air.
When it came time to move, my piano and I were the last to leave.

4

Today there's nothing left.
A giant mustard-yellow box of besser brick commands the site.
Inside its darkness, men make glass.
The land on this side harvests industrial fruit,
the mechanic's muscle, the panel beater's clang,
extending the line started by Stanley Tools
where once a man with steel-hard eyes sold me nails.
Acrylic commerce cements the green,
in sacrifice to hardware – components, parts, supplies
and a fleet of signs crowding the sky.
Opposite a row of houses remains, valiant and defiant
in its freshly-painted, newly-planted insistence.

5

In 1978 old Stan lived up the hill, his yard filled with wood.
We watched his creaky truck lurch its way down to us.
His hair grey and thin, jacket and boots scuffed from years of use,
face pale as he unloaded the ton.
With stiff swings Stan tapped his strength, earned his forty dollars.
I search in vain now for his house, knowing
the whims of supply and demand
greet this memory with a mirror of aluminium and amber glass.

6

The Delishus Café was the place to be.
People travelled the distance north to Albert Road
for apricot strudel and vienna coffee.
Inside the low-lit warmth the smell of soup beckoned.
Women in headscarves and aprons
served with calm, Austrian formality.
The tables dressed in skirts and flowers,
the wall a splash of postcards from Europe,
and quietly, behind the well-mannered chatter,
Strauss waltzed from the cassette player.
At the Delishus you were somewhere else.

7

Across the road the Ladies Rest Room,
for five cents clean toilets, soap and towels.
Women and children welcome to sit away from the traffic
with tea and biscuits for fifty cents,
in the shade of well-kept shrubs and trees.
There were things to buy – marmalade, jam, cakes and cuttings.
The CWA soothed the business of the day.
In the park saplings and plaques
remember Joy, Alison, Marjorie, Edna, Hilary and Mary.

8

We were Luna, Didi, Dragon and Juno.
We breezed about on motorbikes with new ideas
and energetic hope for a better world. Our work
walked the angry road of domestic violence and hardened teenage girls.
At our house in Albert Road
we talked injustice, liberation and the power of language,
womyn not ladies, we turned meaning on its toes.

9

In 1988 I drove Lotus my Beetle
to a cottage in Albert Road painted royal blue and red,
where busy brothers fixed cars.
Later, when Lotus was rammed by a van in the wet
they came running onto Albert Road, to the rescue.
All these years later and four blocks wider,
the business and children have grown.
A tall keep-out fence, metal-electric, warns thieves.
Three young men emerge from the workshop,
olive-brown handsome with celebrity smiles,
the next generation, already arrived.

10

The go-getting dollar says beauty is costly and
there's no time for poetry, unless shouted from a bar.
On Albert Road nasturtiums still climb the timber-yard wall.
Beyond the factories and warehouses, the abandoned junk spaces,
the power-tool scream, the chemical rub,
there's pin-wheel spin, clean white lines and Leunig curl,
colonial mansion, leafy bungalow, or trim sixties brick
enjoying the sounds of Vietnamese radio,
paths hemmed by spring onion and garlic.
Moonah's streets of free verse stand quirky and elegant,
a tapestry sectioned and braided by each boundary fence.

Marion Bay (1)

Dark cliffs embrace her blue expanse
foam frill gushes in the winter light.
Today an icy wind steals my attention,
chills my face. The sun broods behind clouds,
pokes through here and there onto patches
of paddocks and hills laced with trees,
comforts my back like a warm hand.

On other days when the heat
trembles through still air
the inlet mouth smiles a glassy aquamarine,
invites you to picnic on crayfish, celebrate friendship.
The closer you get to the other end, the further away it seems.
I see people walking, silhouette rhythms,
receding to dots,
like the grains of seaweed on the sand.

Marion Bay (2)

A sea of wide-awake, azure blue swollen with a navy-blue shadow beneath its surface. The smell of salt expands my nostrils. I stretch my arms out as if it were possible to embrace this magnificence, stretch on and on as if my finger tips might touch its edges…on a calm, companionably sunny day like this, with that winter freshness still against my cheek, I walk along this huge beach, feel at once big and small, the waves rolling in quite gently, yet I know how tempestuous it can be on other days, but even on a calm day the sea sends mist across the sand.

Over towards the inlet, said to be treacherous, where the boats go out to sea, the aquamarine water laps at my feet in whispers, entices me to plunge its crystal depths. Gulls line up along the edge. Over this way it is so quiet that when I walk I can hear my shoes chew the wet sand.

Hard to believe that at other times a four-wheel drive might blast this silence like a crass advertisement, leaving behind a long scar of tread and the hovering stink of diesel. This is also the place where some like to gather with their vehicles and boats for recreation. What are they re-creating, I wonder, with their need for speed and noise? What impulse pushes them to growl at the quiet and gouge the landscape?

Behind the dunes, near the car park, is a group of shacks. Their on-guard fortress-like appearance seems odd next to the openness of the sea side. Further along, just before the road crosses over that lagoon-like stretch of water known as Blackman Bay on the map, a broken sign says, WARNING DANGEROUS CURRENTS AND… I think of how you might choose to finish this sentence were you the owner of one of those houses standing exposed in its square of space, reinforced by security lights and barbed wire running the length of the fence line.

Across the channel the low hills are dense with trees. A few small, green dwellings merge into the thickness. There's an old jetty so clearly outlined in this light, it seems to be within easy reach, and beneath it a mirror reflection of brown rocks and the tree-thick hills. This is the place to sit and breathe, in and out, slowly, calmly. A boat comes in, the channel stirs and to my left the sea's sunlit jewels dance.

Marion Bay, for me, is a long memory of treasured times spent with friends. Twenty-plus years ago I started walking on this beach with friends: afternoon walks on the weekend with conversation and day-packs, group get-togethers to celebrate birthdays, sunny late morning wanders with our dogs.

Echo and I used to come here regularly when we lived in town. Echo the colour of sand, shone like the sun at Marion Bay, her little brown nose sniffing the air as she walked beside me. When we sat together on the sand she became mesmerised by the pattern and sound of the water, at one with its rhythms, beyond thought but full of knowing, her eyes eventually closing and her head nodding as the fresh air and sea chant sent her to sleep. Later there was Jiggs, a much younger soul even when she became an old dog, who ran up and down bounding with energy, covering twice the distance the rest of us walked, her puppy-like smile in total appreciation of this extraordinary place. I am especially saddened to now know that it was dogs and their careless owners who were responsible for the loss of the bird life here.

I've celebrated a number of birthdays at Marion Bay over the years – I remember once there were about six of us and we came here with baskets full of gourmet picnic goodies, but it was too windy on the beach, so we settled ourselves down into the dunes out of the wind and cheerfully tried to stop our excited dogs from kicking sand onto our food, as we drank champagne and dipped our Turkish bread into hummus. In the dunes the greeny-blue grasses, needle-sharp, are off-set by the soft, white-grey sand. On overcast days the intensity of this blue-green on white-grey is deliciously mellow.

My most recent birthday celebration at Marion Bay happened on an autumn day, warm, still and full of sparkle – a paradise day. We got there late morning and met up with an old friend who'd bought a crayfish on her way back from the peninsula. Three of us sat in the sunshine eating crayfish, rolls and fruit, wearing our good fortune in being here like a new skin. Later we went for a walk towards the northern end of the beach, each of us stopping at different points for a rest and each of us from a distance, looking like tiny bits of coloured seaweed hardly visible, marvellously insignificant against nature's immense backdrop.

Today I am the only person on this beach, a little blob of red and black on the sand. This is the place I longed for years ago, while sitting on a beach crammed with people, not far from Amsterdam. When I described it to my Dutch friend, she thought the prospect of being on such a big empty beach, terrifying. But I am not alone here. My spirit jumps with glee, as I walk amongst the seaweed drifts and the tufts of rubbery succulent, sprouting tiny purple flowers sturdy as ever in the sand, reminding me it's nearly spring.

Yet in these very moments, as I celebrate Planet Earth's sublimity, I am also acutely aware of the historical price paid by those who once belonged to this place – the bands of the South Oyster Bay people – whose eventual demise shaped the kind of wild emptiness I know as Marion Bay today. When Nicholas Marion du Fresne anchored his ship at North Bay in 1772, the people of the South Oyster Bay area had their first contact with Europeans, and as described in historical accounts, it was ill-fated. The unfortunate clash that occurred resulted in the first killing and wounding of local people by Europeans. Marion du Fresne sailed on to New Zealand where he was killed in a clash with some Maori people. The power of an eighteenth century imperial European heritage that still has us calling this place Marion Bay, after such a short visit by the French navigator, seems astonishing to me. What was the name of this place before Marion came here? So many questions and so many lost answers.

Today at the beginning of the twenty-first century, as I walk along this shore, I absorb mostly its vast naturalness, grateful for the refuge it now provides in a world wrecked by war and environmental vandalism. I watch clouds constantly change shape as they drift over

Maria Island which sometimes looks like a giant, lolling whale. The chequered pattern of farmed hills overlooking the beach, the crisp winter light, the sea's deep breathing at the base of my chest, all tell me something about what matters. Sometimes what matters is the wind when it whips me around – no chance for sitting then. Sometimes what matters is the wrestling that has to be done with the tragic twists and turns of history. Sometimes what matters is the sea flat and lazy, or the cool, damp hardness of the sand. Sometimes it's the deep, green tunnel of wave. Sometimes what matters is the boundless energy in walking forever, it would seem, along these shores, on and on and on, the closer you get to reaching the end, the further away it looks to be.

For there is another kind of emptiness here, that is both nurturing and uplifting. It is not the emptiness born of historical tragedy, nor is it that clichéd 'there's nothing here' emptiness still misunderstood by tourists who favour more crowded spaces. Rather, it is an emptiness that takes me to my centre, and requires a kind of surrender to the landscape, even if for only the time it takes to go for an afternoon walk. An openness to a deeper organic pulse that somehow transcends mere physicality and gives me an insight into what it is to be human, beyond words, beyond the demands and routines of everyday language and culture.

Today is Monday. Worldly success, for me, is being here on a Monday if I want to be. I look at this place and hope the fly-by tourists will find it too cold, too quiet, too outdoors. I hope the get-rich-quick developers who don't like taking no for an answer, will be swallowed up by the bond of land and water. Freedom for me, is not wanting the pizzazz that has you win and others lose. Success for me, is an on-going conversation between work and play, getting beyond the separation. In absorbing this big, yawning, late-afternoon beach as the sun heads for the hills, I feed on its exquisitely creative atmosphere. The sharply silhouetted hills feature the few remaining trees on top. They look like a display of paper cut-out decorations against a sky awash with crimson. I head back over the dunes, take in a last glimpse of the sea; as usual it is difficult to leave.

At Bicheno

1

This place feeds memory
in water-wash across a lap of stone,
framed by that line luminous and beckoning,
perfect because it does not exist.
Once feared by ships,
there in sharp relief
as elusive as definition gets,
it stretches eternal on the edge of imagination.

The pull and sway
of old-mother hips laden with kelp
soothe my fears.
The rush and swash of each fresh wave
and the distant trill of gulls
comfort my sleep.

The selling of paradise is a cliché,
real-estate make believe,
for those who like to get in quick,
Life's a Beach. On the sand one tiny shell spectacular,
its minute cone hemmed in stripes
black and white like a zebra –
takes you to Africa *en plein air*.

2

Sparkle filled the morning like a promise,
so much generosity was always going to seem
unreal in the end. Still it was enough.
By afternoon the steel-grey swell
cast all that dazzle, pirouetting on a cheerful sea,
as if it were days ago.

The journey south – up, down, up and over,
a rock-ballet – jump, stretch, strain, tip, hop,
past houses of grand design
and tinted glass like blindness,
jutting, oddly outcast, vacant on the point, missing it,
the short-lived romance an impulse.

In the drying, low-tide summer,
apricot granite smooth as pumice pampers
kelp-crunching feet rinsed pure in brine.
Near clefts of fungi stench and penguin death,
mysterious like sin,
bleached bones lie untouched by fire,
relics of flight that once graced the sky.

I read each curve of the coast,
past the scrub in my head, past the cave of thought,
another chapter of erosion and contour,
sure to be scuttled by the next high tide.
Out there the line of purple pales to white
in the face of mountain rain
despite the limits of vision,
darkness links to light

In a pool Neptune's necklace swirls
lazy on the incoming surge,
crabs scurry to the shade,
sea-lettuce flashes its transparent skirt.
Veins of quartz recall a liquid past,
sediment seasoned and baked
its scent the start of all I know.
Like an old lover, this place wraps me
in the soaking fullness of myself.

Myrtle Shadows and Jigsaw Clouds

In the mystery-maze of memory and time, I am learning that the longer I live, the more likely it is I'll forget much of what I've done in the past, so that returning to a place can feel like experiencing it anew. Without memory, how can we know who we've been or how we got to be who we are today? And how random is memory? How much of it relies on prompts such as photos or other people who've shared an experience of time and place. Even then the accounts would vary.

I've been to Cradle Mountain about six times in thirty years. I think that surely I must have come here during my first two years of living in Tasmania (1978–1980) but if I did, I don't remember and there are no photos.

My first memory time here was with my parents in 1984. We came to Cradle Mountain as part of a two-week holiday drive around Tasmania. The second memory time is a rainy weekend in a group of six friends, four of us from Hobart and two from interstate – we danced carefree in the Ballroom Forest and got soaking wet. The next time was with Kath and Carol (before she worked here) in the mid-1990s. I'm shocked to realise that it could quite possibly be nearly a decade since I was last here.

The Cradle Mountain infrastructure has since become more sophisticated. Like the other parks that attract lots of tourists there is now a formal fee-paying visitors' centre, whereas before walkers and campers simply stopped in at the ranger's office. The campground that used to be just inside the park no longer exists and has been replaced by one situated off the road just before the official park entrance. A shuttle bus goes from the visitors' centre to Dove Lake. The track circumnavigating the lake is completely constructed of boards and mesh. The Waldheim Huts have twenty-four-hour electricity, gas heaters and fridges, stoves and ovens. The tracks are better maintained.

This afternoon I meet all kinds of people: some who are excited at being here for the first time; some who have come to paint; some who ask me how long it takes to walk around Dove Lake; others, who possibly don't walk much, talk about how tired they are after the two-hour circuit. Then there are the people who shouldn't come here – like the person who left orange peel on a clump of button grass.

Many people, it seems, are walking as quickly as they can. I don't understand them. Why walk in such a hurry in a place like this? Is it some kind of test? Are they seeing anything? Are they anxious – wanting to do the circuit but, at the same time, eager to get away from the wildness? They speed past all the different plants, the whisper of the lake, the bird talk and the squeak of trees stretching their limbs. If you slow down, this wonder is all there for the absorbing.

I ease my body into its rhythm which is steady rather than fast. Dove Lake walkers used to wind their way around its perimeter along a rocky path plaited with tree roots and boggy in places. The boardwalk now protects all this and makes it a different experience – it's more like drifting around the lake. My mother would have enjoyed the ease of this new track.

*

I settle into the pleasant little cabin called Binya one of the group of Waldheim cabins that are a kind of tribute to Gustav and Kate Weindorfer who built the original chalet here, now a museum.

A three-quarter moon with a rainbow halo illuminates jigsaw clouds. In the thick quiet outside, I feel the island's pulse where the pencil pines and myrtle beech shape the shadows of this mild night.

Inside Binya the sounds of the kettle, the gas heater, the fridge and Segovia on the tape player keep me company. I turn off the fluorescent light and turn on the bedside lights for a warmer glow.

Gustav Weindorfer spoke of a unique kind of luxury when he said *This is Waldheim where there is no time and nothing matters...* The moonlight, like a trusty companion, comes through my window and onto my left shoulder.

*

In the morning the sun warms my back as I listen to Chopin and wait for the porridge to cook. I anticipate the day's walk across the button grass and up to Marion's Lookout, then down to Dove Lake and back again.

The floor of Cradle Valley shimmers with button grass that, in the autumn sunlight, looks like green-gold pincushions. Behind me the Waldheim rainforest dense with king-billy pine, myrtle beech, celery-top pine, mop pandanus and other species, looks like a fantasy forest. When a landscape like this is allowed to be itself, we have the privilege of seeing it at its full potential. The cattle country just outside the park is a complete contrast. Cattle have their place – as a beef-eater I fully appreciate this fact – but, in the wrong place, there's no denying the damage they do to the landscape.

In the deep blue sky a red helicopter dangles its load of planks as it travels back and forth to some place beyond the Horse Track where maintenance is underway. I think of Carol up here, the hard-work fun she must have had and the many tracks she has worked on – I'm instantly impressed by the skill that as gone into the track I'm walking on today, every bit of it worth my annual park fees.

*

The day is just right for walking: clear, sunny, warm to cool, no wind. I pass many tourists busy with cameras. I walk to Crater Lake down the hill from where Carol, Kath and I walked to Crater Peak along the Horse Track. I follow the path over the sparkle of gushing creeks, through myrtle forest, then climb a stairway and pass waterfalls that look like those featured in wilderness photography. Each time I see such waterfalls I'm amazed that they are actually like that: places of picture-book enchantment, their mist replenishing and cool.

I stop by the boatshed at cosy Crater Lake, remembering the day I stopped here with my parents, realising again and appreciating more acutely, the climbing my mother did here for the first time at the age of sixty-four. Dad was fifty-six and I was twenty-nine. The weather was cool and changeable, even though it was January. Mum and Dad stood with their backs to the camera as they paused to gaze upwards at the prominent blue-grey stone that forms Crater Peak on one side of the lake and Wombat Peak on the other, emerging from the mist. I know my father loved it; I hope my mother at least enjoyed the scenery and didn't find it too gloomy. I was sharing my world with them, I wanted them to be as taken with it as I was and I took that photo because I enjoyed seeing my parents in a place that was special to me. Today I'm not far off the age my father was then. The wind coming across the water is still icy but the slopes above the lake are golden with fagus gleaming in the sun.

I make my way up the side of Wombat Peak and come to the ridge that overlooks Dove Lake. The day the three of us made it up to this point my parents were standing in the drizzle with their rainjackets and hoods on as we looked across at Hanson's Peak. I wonder what they were thinking as the visibility lessened. I hope my mother was doing more than persevering, that she wasn't simply 'cold and miserable' as I heard a woman today describe her previous experience here.

I continue up a well-built, almost vertical set of stony steps – the steepest part of the Overland Track – to Marion's Lookout, where the view is resplendent. All those overused superlatives that as a writer you try to avoid, come rushing to my mind as I stand here.

The place is busy with tourists from other parts of Australia. They've come for the views. They share their on-top-of-the-world amazement and bravado as they discover this place for the first time, some bragging about all the other tracks they've done as if there were a kind of competition. Like other iconic World Heritage sites, this one also draws the crowds, upwards of 200,000 per year. Twenty-five years ago there weren't nearly so many people. The noise of helicopters comes and goes taking the track timber to other precipitous places. I decide that it was just as well it was misty that time my mother was here, as she would not have been able to climb this far up and she might have tried, and the attempt might have gone wrong.

I sit to the side by myself and marvel at the close-up jaggedness of Cradle Mountain, as well as the view of the Great Western Tiers and Mount Roland in the distance. Words quickly become superfluous in places like this: not up to the task of naming or describing, they recede to the background. Better to listen to the poetry of the wind and dwell on the sense of one's minute place in this vast spread of ancient life.

A day like this tempts me to stay on and on as I cast my eye over this country of seemingly endless tracks and peaks. But after a while, I start back down the slope, pausing just below Marion's Lookout to dwell on the perfect shape of Lake Lilla.

Further on as I descend the step-track, I pass a group of young women strong with large packs starting out on the Overland Track. They remind me of myself thirty years ago and I fancy they might camp tonight at Twisted Lakes. Although I feel more like a local than I used to because I can direct people and I know the names of certain landmarks, this will always be a place I am getting to know – its moods tell me something different every time. I consider Carol's sense of knowing this place when, as a ranger, she spent months walking the length of the Overland Track back and forth.

Dove Lake is coffee brown with a crema edge, like the brown in my father's photo that he took at dusk from Face Track. Up too high when he shouldn't have been and finishing the lake circuit in the dark, my father was here on his own that time. He never wore a watch, he would have been outside time and totally entranced by the landscape.

Angles are deceiving: from down the slope Marion's Lookout appears higher than Cradle peak. I pass people fiddling with their cameras, heads down, missing the majestic hillside of trees above them.

Do we capture on film what we think we see? Perhaps it's too much to take in all this at once. At Wombat Pool I contemplate the ancient elegance of pencil pine reflections on olive-brown water and try to visualise this place thousands of years ago.

Toward the end of the day, Marion's Lookout catches the last of the sun and I see myself up there exposed at this late hour. I cross back through the valley now in shadow. The sharp chill in the evening air reminds me of the power this place commands. A sunset raven has the last word – is it the raven of thought or memory? The atmosphere immediately softens on entering the shelter of the Waldheim forest where I am greeted by the chirp of a green rosella and the busy twittering of small birds.

*

The next morning Cradle Mountain is hiding in the fog, disappointing those tourists who've dropped by for a quick look. The mist makes cameras flash, mutes distant colours, illuminates closer ones.

I head up the Lake Rodway Track towards Hanson's Peak. I come without glasses, hat or camera, feeling raw from a nightmare that woke me with my sobbing – a kind of premonition about trees chopped down and our old house exposed to a newly built suburb.

I sit surrounded by burnt-orange fagus and the peaceful slopes of Lake Hanson remembering how we walked to this place twenty-four years ago, via Hanson's Peak. Looking at its incline I can hardly believe we did that – I can't remember the descent in detail but I do remember being proud of my mother's efforts, even though underneath I was concerned. Her body was working hard and she asked my father and me what she was doing in a place like this and why we had brought her here. After the descent she sat grim-faced, perhaps worrying that her heart was about to give out. We were still up very high, on a walk officially rated these days by the Visitors' Centre as difficult. My mother sat resting with her back to us, looking out at this same view, though higher up than I am now. She wanted us to leave her alone. The fagus was green but back then I didn't know it was fagus.

I didn't know as much as I do now about judging walks and fitness and taking risks. Older, wiser and more careful, I appreciate how determined my mother was in coming with us as I discover my own limits to strength and courage. I hope there was something about being here that inspired her. The photo of her high up here looking over the slopes around Mount Campbell and Lake Hanson is one of my favourites because, in my preferred version of the story, she was enjoying the experience of wildness. This same photo probably reminded her of nothing more than a frightening, difficult trek. She never came back here or anywhere else to do this kind of walking, though later on she seemed to enjoy showing the photos to her relatives who thought her brave.

I wanted my mother to love this place like I did, but things were not that simple or straightforward. In those days we wanted one another to be different kinds of people. It would take another nine years before I came to a deeper understanding of our mutual love and loyalty for one another.

The fagus on the slopes of Mount Campbell is the same colour as my jacket and I feel absorbed into its orangeness. A man comes down from Hanson's Peak pausing to tell me of his annoyance at his flat camera batteries and at last year's heavy rain that stripped the fagus bushes of their leaves. He keeps going.

The morning mist has lifted. The side view of Cradle Mountain from this point reveals its three-peak shape, telling me that the postcard, face-on view of the two-peaked cradle is but one perspective.

Kelly's Steps

Salamanca Place, Hobart
After *Kelly's Steps* by Chen Ping

The morning drizzles blue,
he shivers in the ghost cold,
stuck in a muffled dream of loss,
in a place he thought he knew.
He hears her voice from long ago
coming from the blue shadow of memory
don't bring me this way again –
sharp against a peculiar dis/ease
she felt creeping around her shoulders
that day, even in the sun. The mood
now is framed by a slash of yellow light
around the charcoal gloom of the steps
ahead, another point of departure.

Beneath a Wild Tangle

Green oh how I love you green.
Green wind. Green boughs…

Beneath the gypsy moon
things are looking at her…

> from 'Sleep Walking Ballad' by Federico Garcia Lorca

I

There is an old house on ten acres of land tucked into the foot-hills of Mount Wellington. I've lived in many places but this was where I experienced the most contentment and where I developed a deep, affectionate sense of place.

Woven in story, this particular place is threaded to a distant past still strongly felt. I try to imagine who belonged to this land, who lived there, wandered through it, long before houses and cleared hills when the people of the Mouheneenner band were its custodians. John Glover's paintings show this area thick with trees right down to the shores of what we know as the River Derwent.

Since the early 1830s the story of this house has been one of many chapters. The old title tells us, for example, that in those days the land attached to the house consisted of a hundred acres which was granted to Thomas Wells and Henry Bilton in 1825 by the Lieutenant Governor of Tasmania, Colonel George Arthur. Reformed bush-ranger Martin Cash bought that and another sixty acres in the 1830s, and lived there with his convict wife Mary Bennett, who out-lived both their son and her infamous husband. An arrangement by Cash before his death saw the land passed on to John Pregnall. Later, in 1910, Margaret McShane sold it to William Pierce. Back then, the land across the road was owned by Annie O'Brien. Who were these women Margaret McShane and Annie O'Brien that they were able to own land? An early photo of the house shows an enormous pear tree close to its front, probably part of Cash's orchard, the remnants of which still grace the garden. As well as growing fruit trees, he grazed cattle on the high slopes, now a reserve known as Goat Hills. Martin Cash's hundred acres, it seems, would have stretched along the whole side of the creek up and down the road, and over the top. Since then many people have lived there – some I know about, but most remain unknown to my partner and me. Our chapter spanning the past twenty-two years, focuses on the land, the weather, the animals and how we were shaped by this intimate experience of nature.

Surrounded by bush, the house gladly merges with its natural environment, invites it in, breathes its perfumes, moves with it. In the room that was my study, quarter-pane windows stretch around its two sides, facing onto gums, wattles, an old elderberry, a pittosorum, a blackwood and a towering pine on the other side of the creek planted by a woman now in her nineties. The creek runs beside the road and is bordered by crack willows. These should be removed and probably will one day. The blackberries should also go but, for now, they stabilise the bank and, when they fruit, make tasty sauce. Opposite my desk, in the summer, kookaburras sat on the gum branches waiting for skinks and blue tongues to make the wrong moves. Through these windows I often watched the creek rippling its water, clean and sparkling from spring rain or listened to it roaring at full volume in the winter. But for most of the past thirteen years, the creek was dry. Like others aware of the future likelihood of drier, warmer weather, I hoped for significant rain. Finally in 2009 the rain came again, months and months of it, to everyone's astonishment. After this much rain the creek becomes the rivulet it really is – Islet Rivulet – its water bounteous, fast-flowing, deep, its adult voice gushing strong and loud like a waterfall, the sunlight dancing a surface pattern of sparkle and shadow. After days of rain and mist, the whole place wakes up refreshed; I'd open all the doors and windows, put on Schubert's *Trout* Quintet, rejoice.

I felt a great sense of fortune in living there – it was as if I was meant to be there, something I'd only realised after a number of years. At times I dreamt I was no longer there, that it was no longer my place to live in, and in this dream I felt a devastating loss, not just of a house but of a deep sense of home – the loss felt irreplaceable. In the dream no-where else felt right. And yet we always knew one day we would leave that place. Choosing to end a good relationship is fraught. The risk of regret confronts the desire for change. At times, we've hardly been able to think about it.

When I told my mother twenty-two years ago that I was moving there, she exclaimed half-indignantly, 'Montrose!' with her Scottish emphasis on the second syllable, for the original Montrose is not far from my place of birth in Scotland. The general area at the back of Glenorchy, a suburb of Hobart named after Glen Orchy the Scottish district west of Perth, has three names – Montrose, Rosetta, Berriedale. It's hard to know where one area ends and the other begins. We lived all that time in a neck of bush at the end of a no through road. Despite a small subdivision further up on the other side, our neighbourhood was still, more or less, like a country valley, still a corner beneath trees alive with bird calls.

The subdivision transformed the hill where wild goats used to wander. In their place stand about twenty contemporary brick houses. I call this cluster of houses a twenty-first century village. It sits alongside the house on the hill built in the 1920s with a grand view of the river, and our old house built in bits and pieces over the years from about the 1830s onwards. The house further down the road was also probably built in the 1920s. These old houses surrounded by acreage create a buffer that makes this valley the place it is. I like to think the more recent residents value the presence of the bush on the hill and the feeling of peace it brings. Sometimes I'm not sure if they do.

When you walk over to that twenty-first century side of the road, walk up its neat concrete footpath, see the neat lawns and landscaped gardens, you feel as if you are in a totally different world. At the top of its hill the road peters out to bush and scrub again. The houses stand close together, their people are largely invisible to us, we don't know them, we hardly see them. Most residents enter and exit the valley by car. These new houses brought a sealed road and more cars; and an end to the dust and mud from the old dirt road; the cars travel faster, too fast most of the time. The new houses have also brought an interesting sort of suburban silence, punctuated by the sounds of cars coming and going at either ends of the day, a few barking dogs, the squeals of children, the rumble of lawnmowers and the intrusiveness of other people's parties in the summer. Despite the close proximity of the houses, there is a privacy it seems – people mind their own business, stay polite with one another, friendly but not too friendly. A politeness that creates its own kind of closed, inside space. There looks to be little chance for outside privacy in the village, little chance to expose your windows without a veil.

The slopes on the bush side of the valley are steeper, darker and more upright. Our former cottage at the bottom is protected by these slopes. It looks tiny – nestled beneath trees, you can hardly see it. On Google Earth it looks like a speck of white in a sea of green. The trees, the ten acres, the land along that side of the creek are a cocoon of green on the edge of the city. The twenty-three acre grassy hill across the road, with its beautiful house, has long been zoned 'future urban' and finally, after all these years, there's a plan for a subdivision of fifty-three houses.

Some say this is 'progress'. Some say this is the way of the world. Will the developer get his way while exploiting the notion of 'bush ambience'? A notion that will add dollar value to any new blocks of land, even though this same bush – the bulk of our former ten acres – is worth little in real estate terms because it is zoned conservation, it is steep and it can't be easily cut down or cut up. Paradoxically it is both valuable and valueless. Will an era of climate change and collapsing global capital sufficiently challenge these notions of value? In another ten to twenty years, if we have any species survival-sense left by then, this kind of land, with its trees breathing oxygen into our terminal atmosphere, should become priceless.

There used to be bush all the way down the road to another historic home: Montrose House. Then with what seemed like incredible speed, developers cleared the bush, piped in the creek, built about seventy houses along and back up the hill, all brick houses, some large and showy, most built very close together. It was overwhelming to see the place where I used to walk, so quickly transformed into suburb.

I always wanted to live in an old house and so there I was for twenty-two years, happily in our crooked little piece of patchwork comfort, not overly renovated – a 'character cottage' in real estate parlance. However, in the scheme of things I'm probably selfish – although I love my bush space, I've never wanted to live in a country town or in complete isolation – a cottage in the bush, yes; but with the benefits of a small city close by, a small capital city no less. I too like a certain amount of anonymity, convenience and urban stimulation, as well as the bush. In Hobart it is still possible to find these pockets of urban bushland, but they are constantly at risk of being built-out.

At the end of the road is Wellington Park and a steep walking track called Montrose Trail, said to be built during World War II. It climbs steadily to an area at the top of the surrounding hills where it branches out in all directions: to Collinsvale, to the tower that identifies the hill from a distance, to tracks leading back towards the city end of the mountain, to the council tip in the next valley. I often walked up a section of this track and back home, a return trip of about fifty minutes. The bush along this bit of Islet Rivulet is healthy and reasonably unspoiled. These days it is protected by its Park status, the gate at the end of the road and the fact that it is a steep walk. A short way up the track on the northern bank of the creek, two memorial stones tell us of a brother and sister who, apparently, once lived there. Other signs of past life include a rusted car body dating back to the 1940s by the look of it. At first this wreck looked ugly; now it's weathered, twisted, chocolate-brown rust is like a surreal sculpture that is gradually being swallowed by the green.

This track is rubbish-free, a contrast to the bush along the side of the road below the gate which is regularly littered with rubbish sometimes from cars, sometimes from pedestrians and sometimes it seems to come from the nearby houses. I've never been able to understand why people, some with pinch-neat lawns, think nothing of there being rubbish in the bush, or of bringing their rubbish after dark from somewhere else and dumping it in the creek.

II

Around the old house the moods of the garden change with the seasons. In spring the green grass is the backdrop to red, crimson, purple, yellow, blues, maroons and sepia pinks. The birds gossip endlessly. In wetter years the native hens come out to play and splash. Remarkably a few puddles in the creek still entice the chanting frogs.

In summer the house fills with the sounds and smells of the outside. You have to keep an eye out for smoke. The spring wet dries out, the grass turns into a field of long white daisies, then the green fades and turns to yellow as the clay cracks open like a miniature earthquake.

Come autumn, the ground turns to toasted gold and the leaves from the immigrant trees catch the light, in splashes of yellow, brown, red and orange. Later in the season, the leaves fall and scatter abstract colour across the ground. The afternoon shadows come sooner, fixing the white, green and gold of house and garden into satisfying tones of contrast and well-being.

On a sunny winter's morning there the colour is gum grey-blue and deep blackwood green, crossed with the lively dark brown pattern of knobbly deciduous tree branches that frame the house as in a fairy tale. Winter is the time for withdrawal and solitude, for thinking, dreaming and remembering. Occasionally the snow comes to settle around the house bringing with it a gleaming white delight.

Winter also brings the fog. The mist from the river settles in amongst the hills, blurring boundaries, creating an edgeless universe. Everything's quieter, cars go by more slowly, poking their headlights through its formless curtain like in a Clarice Beckett painting. Where will it lead us this fog, will we lose ourselves? The fog holds our secrets, hides the city, hides our life from view, all that we thought solid, disappears. Then when the fog lifts, the magic and mystery give way to clarity. Everything looks cleaner than before, moist and soft. The birds start to chatter again, the sun warms in spots, and the spiderwebs sparkle with droplets all the way up the hill. Life continues, but you remember the silence of the fog, the silence that tells you things. The silence that wraps a soft coating of tranquillity around your soul, pacifies your thoughts, sets you at ease. This is the gift of fog. This is the promise of a lost world.

III

When you stay in a place long enough you watch a garden outgrow itself. The story of the garden immediately around the house is an epic: its fortunes were our fortunes. The kind of story that might find a place in a gardening magazine full of loving, folksy detail about flowers and vegetables, saplings turning into adult trees, the hours and hours of planting, shaping and maintaining. The heritage-listed fruit trees. The former vegetable garden now replanted with whatever is unappetising to wildlife. The clay. The bank. The paddock. The slope upwards. The land slip. The rocks. The need to mow and cut, rake and sweep. The wind, the leaves, the sticks. The numerous birds, the lizards, the snakes, the wallabies, the pademelons and potoroos, the possums.

In 1987 you might have seen a wallaby once a year. The road now features a sign warning motorists of their presence. The early mornings and late evenings are danger times. Car drivers need to take more care. There is too much roadkill.

The population of marsupials is there to stay. At dusk and dawn they make their way up and down the hill, babies in their pouches, as they munch on the grass and anything else that takes their fancy. The possums carry their young on their backs over to the compost heap or up trees close to the house. The birds also became more numerous and of a wider variety than they once were. Just before we left, a currawong couple hatched a chick high in the fork of the peppermint gum near the corner of the house. The place has became a wildlife sanctuary.

Most of the ten acres spans the slope at the northern side of the house and is a tangle of trees, sticks and rocks. Animal tracks wind through its thicket at a criss-cross of angles, a crazy pattern all of its own. A crazy mess of life: you come across an old bit of fence – a stick on the ground with rusted wires attached; birds watch you and call out; a wallaby thumps here and there as you clamour and climb through it all, a few steps this way then that way, as you look and stop again, trying to find the easiest route, watching out for slippery sticks, prickles and thorns, as you walk through spiderwebs. The bush falls and grows over itself, breeds saplings everywhere: wattle, blackwood, gum, she-oak. Messy, messy, not tidy, uncontrollable and thriving. Despite the drier climate and the subsequent loss of many trees over the past thirteen years, the bush continued to renew itself.

What can it mean 'to own' a wild tangle of bush like this – to walk around and through it, and say 'this is our land'? When you are in amongst it, you feel that it embraces you, that it 'owns' you. How impossible the idea of ownership seems in this context. When we first moved there someone asked me what we were going to do with the land. Enjoy it, I answered with some surprise, as if this were not self-evident. This patch of bush was once tamed a little when domestic animals grazed on it. People have tried to control it and many who 'own' bush want to leave their mark. When their attempts fail, the marks left behind amount to rubbish: beer cans, bits of car engine, old window frames, planks of wood, unfinished fences, trees chopped down and left. Owning bush – an independent, complex life force – feels somehow outside the normal sense of owning something, even when you are the title holder. We 'owned' that land in that we looked after it by ensuring it continued to be itself. Around the house, where the land is domesticated, the signs of ownership in the European sense are more obvious but still the land is only superficially tamed. Left to its own devices, nature could easily take over again.

The question of value and what something is worth. The question of money and how it distorts the notion of value. That this place is both valuable and valueless in monetary terms, yet extremely valuable to the natural health of this valley and the future of our planet, simply exposes the skewed logic of economic fundamentalism. Meanwhile, the currawongs are busy feeding their chick.

IV

What makes a house a home? Our old house was alive with creaks and cracks; it was home to animals living underneath, spiders that lived in its walls and came out to catch flies in the summer. Possums screeched and clattered over the roof at night. Sparrows, wrens, fantails, finches, honeyeaters and eastern spinebills searched continuously for nesting places. It was home to dogs and cats. It's a tranquil house and it likes to take its time. It was my principal place of work, I spent most days there feeling blessed by the creative opportunities it gave me.

Choosing to leave meant we ended this blessed chapter in our lives and just like in saying goodbye to an old friend for the last time, we may have left a part of ourselves behind. We contemplated this difficult choice for over a year before making our decision. My journal is full of grief about it. The sadness will continue to leak out of me. Yet the tangle of probabilities that led to our move remain.

Most people who visited that place remarked on its beauty, peace and comfort. It was an honour and a privilege to live there – it gave us so much freedom, even while it demanded energy and responsibility. The slopes and curves of the land provided many angles from which to look at the world. The house caressed and nurtured us. Through its windows or from the land's corners, passageways and banks, you can look up, down, across and over, never seeing the same thing twice.

The Hill

She looks across at the hill
from where she's come
after all these years, months, weeks, days, hours.
She imagines
a flock of white cockatoos rasping
the eucalypt air, pictures
the morning veranda empty,
the leaf-laced windows no longer
her point of view,
not quite believing
the official, legal facts,
of displacement.

Leaving Lake St Clair

Picture a morning: grey, drizzly-damp, muted bird noises, I wake up with the urge to get moving after a night of restlessness, annoyed at the lack of sleep. I have breakfast, I pack, I leave my friend-the-ranger's house, call into the visitor's centre to drop off the key on my way out. The drizzle continues. By the time I hurry back to the car – all of two minutes – I notice the drizzle on my windscreen has ice in it. Better to leave now the duty ranger said to me with a knowing smile. The snow was on its way to five hundred metres. No view of the peaks this morning. The grey is getting thicker and darker.

*

My imagination is too fertile for my own good at times. Forty-five minutes later out on the road I see the sleet coming across in thick white sheets. Little explosions of ice hit at my window from all directions. Cars coming towards me have their lights on. How far down is five hundred metres, I wonder as I feel panic lurking around the edges of my intelligence, how fast can weather travel? Weather controls things, weather controls time. How high or low is five hundred metres, I wonder again as the sheet of sleet continues to travel across the flat. How fast can weather make me stuck in snow? Ten minutes, half an hour? How long before the roads are closed? How long before I'm stuck in the cold not able to go forward or back? Just stuck with no mobile phone. A mobile phone probably wouldn't work in these conditions, a mobile phone would be useless. I'd just be stuck with snow piling up around me, no doona in the boot, no flask of hot tea, everything freezing and me turning into a cold corpse.

I think of the thick snow of Scotland I've seen. I think of the spring blizzard that we drove through in Nebraska where cars veered off the road in front of us. And here I was practically in my own spring blizzard. Alone. Ah! There's that house surrounded by all the junked cars and trucks – I could call in there for shelter. No, I'd probably get murdered. Anyone who has all those wrecks for a garden is bound to be a murderer. Stupid! Why didn't you listen for the road weather alert? All those road weather alerts – like 'road closed between Derwent Bridge and Tarraleah'. Am I driving on a road that will soon be closed? How soon? How quickly does weather travel? How high or low is five hundred metres?

*

The music I've turned on for comfort is no comfort: Hayden's Cello Concerto is suitably menacing in this atmosphere but it's better than silence. Anxiety is flooding through me, filling my veins with jelly concentrate. I'm driving at speed along a road that's soon to be closed. The cello's moan takes a dive. Breathe deeply, breathe deeply, breathe, breathe. The jelly is in my legs. My feet are getting cold. Breathe. Don't let this take over. You need to think straight, drive straight. My legs and arms hurt, my stomach aches. Breathe, breathe. Shit – a panic attack!

*

The sleet eases, I can slow my wipers down. Breathe. I am breathing! But everything hurts. No more cello. I turn on the radio. Margaret Throsby's calm voice crackles through. The road starts to descend. The weather eases even more. I stop the car and hoist the aerial higher. Margaret Throsby is coming through loud and clear now and she's talking to a writer who lives in Portugal. The road continues to descend, the weather continues to clear. The sleet is behind me. Margaret Throsby and the writer are talking about Portugal.

*

Portugal! Listening to them, suddenly I'm back in Portugal. And I remember this same physical feeling of anxiety when I was there travelling alone. I controlled it. I controlled it like hell because I was determined to travel. And I'd chosen to do it alone. Margaret Throsby says that Portugal seems like a romantic country to her. Yes, yes, that's what I thought. I wanted it to be romantic. But try being a young woman travelling alone in Portugal in 1981, with romantic notions of cobblestone streets. Portugal nearly drove me mad, but that's another story. But the jelly-like, knotty anxiety was there and I controlled it. But my body felt like steel. Controlling anxiety took its toll. Amelia Rodriguez on the radio now. Ah yes, I know how to pronounce her name, Margaret. I learnt the language, the hard way. I start to imagine sending this writer my essay on Portugal.

*

My stomach aches, thanks to my fertile imagination. If I'd stayed a week instead of a few days at Lake St Clair, I could have watched the snow fall gently through my window while the fire warmed my back. Watch it fall and settle and calm everything to a hush. Can't have a romantic moonlight walk in the snow – on demand – and expect to be able to drive out, as you like, the next morning. I have now driven down past the hydro station and up the other side of the valley. The weather is changing.

*

Sun! Can you believe this place with blue skies and sheep grazing contentedly on green hillsides? Back there in the sleet, cows were huddled together by the fence-line along the road, trying to get away from it all. Sun. Sun. God, can you believe this? My imagination starts to thaw. God, I've got a headache. If I didn't cry so much, I'd be a good candidate for an ulcer. Was I a fool or what? What kind of crazy, wild place in my head did I just travel through? In this part of the world, everything in its picturesque, mild, pre-spring state seems happy. My body still aches from all the adrenalin it created, I feel like I've run a marathon. One thing I don't want to be is a panic merchant. But where was I really, back there in that frenzied, imaginative place?

*

Back there – has the snow come and settled, is Lake St Clair looking like a heavenly, pristine scene from a Dombrovskis card, all at peace after the squall? Are people playing and smiling in the snow? Will they get a romantic, full-blue-moon-in-Pisces walk in the snow without me?

Mount Field Shadows

Explore the undergrowth
life at the bottom is rich, bosky-damp
the lime light soothes
as you awaken to oxygen's kiss.
Photos by the fallen swamp gum
mark your fairy size. Velvet-moss tangle, tree fern giants
confide in riffle creek companion.
Tourists read the signs
huddle on the bridge revived
by the cataract's drifting spray.
Potoroos scurry into the bower
behind picture-pretty myrtle and long-legged laurel.
Nearby a platypus hides in the gurgle
as the faintest shadow of yourself moves ahead on the path.

Three Jewels

I make my way to the Shelf along the duckboards that protect the iced puddles underneath. It's midday and I'm rugged up against the sharp wind. Even in summer, the wind and clouds can carry ice. Today's walking time is curtailed by the probability of a cold-to-freezing change at any moment. Near the dayshelter in a spot of sun below the wind, I look across to the three tarns glittering like jewels. The surrounding fagus is a grey ghost of itself with the merest hint of leftover gold snug against the dark green slopes of the Rodway Range. The track will lead me through rocks covered in black, orange and grey lichen that seems to come alive in the May light.

May is his month, he would have been eighty-two this year. When my father came to the Tarn Shelf all those years ago by himself he was fifty-nine and I worried about him getting lost or having a heart attack. Instead, he felt exhilarated here and experienced freedom for the first time in too many years. He loved the silence that welcomes solitude, away from the hurly-burly of people, timetables, things to do, the crowded, consuming life. He went to Rodway Range, K Col, Naturalist Peak, Mount Field West. He said the wind roared like a train over the ridge at Newdegate Pass. I imagine him walking around these places lost in his secret thoughts, pausing near trickle-water sounds.

The mist moves in over the ridges falling, rising and rolling languidly like a fine curtain in the breeze, before cascading down the cliff towards Lake Seal. I keep trusting it will not turn into fog. Here weather-watching is important. I expect afternoon showers from the west, as forecast. Nearby I hear a gaggle of people's voices on the path somewhere beyond the curve of rocks and interweaving bushes, then overhead a squeaky cacophony of green rosellas. On days like this, you don't linger. I continue but then, about ten minutes later, the clouds travelling quickly crossways convince me to turn back.

Soon I am descending the sixty-degree, four-wheel drive track that services the ski-lodges, gaining momentum as I go, slightly giddy and keenly aware of my knees and thighs – I feel as if I could fly. The ring of the thermos knocking against the side of my pack marks time. Thick grey cloud like dirty cotton wool blankets the sky.

Below on the shores of Lake Dobson I sit beside my favourite alpine yellow gum, drink ginger tea and listen to the rushing creek behind me. Here the sky's grey soothes. I hear walkers speaking animatedly in French. I hear the creek pouring into the lake beneath the footbridge. I remember that first time I brought my father here. We took a 'short cut' across the moorland to the huts. The vegetation suffered and it took longer that we thought.

*

This place always feels like home. I've been here many times with friends, our meandering conversations as full as the effort it takes to walk. Long-lasting friendships traced along these tracks in groups or in pairs. Photos record some of this: a hot summer's wander with Christmas visitors and a dip in the first tarn; six of us on an autumn walk under rich, pearl-grey cloud that provides the best light for a group portrait. There have been walks with those who endure the steep climb from Lake Dobson only for the sake of what comes afterwards; and other walks with a confidant when we've talked our way across the Shelf and back.

The alpine tarns on the Shelf were cut in the last ice age. Their golden-olive water is home to the platypus and the ancient shrimp. A walker literally takes this sense of geological time in her stride and yet it is overwhelmingly impressive. In mid-autumn when the fagus on the slopes of the Rodway Range is a splash of orange, pilgrims come in homage.

*

The next morning I wake to the confidence of sun streaming through the windows. The clouds have dissipated to fluff but they could easily close in again when you least expect it.

The lapping at the edge of the first shelf tarn is like a familiar welcome, it says *listen*; conversation ceases, even if it's only internal conversation. On a sparkling summer's day when the sun has bitten into my skin, the water is an irresistible temptation that takes my breath away with its icy surprise.

At the second tarn the crunching sound of my eating a biscuit fills my head. My tea cools quickly. Water-flow echoes under rocks against a bird's low-key chirping. A freezing breeze ripples across the tarn's surface and halts the flow of ink in my pen. A bird darts suddenly. A native rat scurries across in front of me

I move on, navigating the rocky path and spotting the cairns that tell me where to go. A disgruntled woman coming the other way calls it a Roman road. I continue on past a stand of twisted trunks with a grey iridescent shine, then up another rise and down another slope, at one point standing aside for a group of elderly men who are walking and talking to each other in rapid excitement as they come towards me.

At the third tarn the only sound is a gurgling somewhere beneath the stones and bird rustle behind the bushes. The silence settles in like a kind of eternity. It invites me to know that all is now. At times like this I've imagined a peaceful death when the last sound might be the distant call of a currawong.

There are little pools of water everywhere, and slopes near and far. Beyond the third shelf tarn is a pool surrounded by a stand of pencil pines that look like they belong in a fairy tale. Squat red berry bushes line the track nearby. Further on, near Lake Newdegate, the track descends to Broad River Valley and passes Lake Webster and the smoothly opaque, olive-grey Lake Seal. This is an ideal summer's day walk when there is plenty of daylight to make the round trip a relaxing one. The wind can't get at you on the valley floor quite as much as it can on the shelf. Years ago I went this way with two friends when the ground was boggy. It pulled on my muscles and all the stray, cranky thoughts hiding out in the corners of my mind, making them clash and bang and spark. We finished the walk that day near the Lake Dobson road under the crack of a summer thunderstorm directly overhead. We cheered, called out, laughing with fright at the lightning show.

This profoundly blessed place, here for longer than any of us. Here before humans existed when the wind, the trees, the rocks, the clouds, the tarns knew everything. How can some of us think such places are not worth preserving? I live in gratitude to all those who cared for this country well before I existed. I have benefited enormously from their connection to and their love of this place: from the Pangerninghe people of the Big River tribe who belonged to this land for tens of thousands of years, to those Europeans who more recently worked to have the area declared a national park in 1916, some of whom went moonlight ice-skating on Lake Fenton.

*

My father must have been astounded when he first came here – to find a place like this so far away from his busy family years and the noise of his siren-screaming neighbourhood. This place whispered something fresh and loving to his soul. He went off exploring, enjoyed a wonderful time on his own. I felt pleased. He'd found something worlds away from the routine of long work hours in Sydney. I was reminded of the person who took our family when we were young to the Wollondilly River in NSW. At Mount Field his spirits were revived, his energy grew youthful, he seemed healthier than I'd seen him in the previous twenty years since his heart attack at the age of forty. He loved staying in the Pandani Hut. I imagined him coming back here to spend days, happily hermit-like, listening to the squeals of black cockatoos, feeling the wake-up chill on his cheeks.

My father sent me all his photos of this place, knowing I'd appreciate what they represented. I see the Tarn Shelf back then, twenty plus years ago, looking the same as it does today with that bit of orange fagus still in the identical spot on the Lake Seal slope. He shared with me his joy in discovering all these places – places that I still haven't been to – where he wandered for days. He was so proud of his panoramic shots of Mount Field East sent with his detailed, slightly mathematical instructions on the back telling me how to join them up. I imagine the track over the moorland full of water holes, all muddy. I can also see what's changed – the track going to the Tarn Shelf before it was all duckboards; the newly renovated Telopea Hut previously closed to walkers; the exteriors of the other huts now considerably weathered. I sense my body is becoming more like my father's body – certainly my legs, like his, are all muscle.

His dream was to come and live in Hobart. But life had other plans. Back in New South Wales the stresses and strains thinned his hair, turned his complexion sickly. I'm sad he's not here now, even though we'd argue about which direction to take.

These thoughts get me to Eagle Tarn near Lake Dobson – not pretty, but at peace with the morning. I see him sitting on the steps of Pandani in 1990 and I think about the hard decade he had ahead of him when the problems peaked. He never got back to this place – he never made it through to the next decade, to this new century. Grief took its toll. I can hear him changing the subject, telling me not to be ridiculous.

*

I follow a heavily wooded, narrow track sloping downwards to Platypus Tarn, a seemingly insignificant tiny pool tucked in behind Lake Seal. It skirts tall gums, banksias and waratah. Below I stand at the tarn's muddy bank, it looks stagnant and I wonder if there are indeed platypuses swimming in it. In a corner, thread-like reeds catch the sun's light as they curl out of the water. I feel hemmed in by the dense conical steepness surrounding me. Here the solitude is unsettling, the stillness a little scary, there is a heaviness to the water. I walk back up the hill, those little yellow tree markers my psychological anchor. I remember hearing Les Murray on the radio saying that country people don't go into the bush for pleasure like urban walkers do, but settle on its perimeter instead. Is this where a certain kind of hostility towards the bush comes from: a fear of its density, of getting lost in it, of it swallowing you, of the possibility of falling limbs, of the yawning trees and the ghost-like murmuring? As soon as I reach higher ground and the woods thin out, this sense of foreboding lifts.

Back at Lake Dobson the mood is breezy and pleasant. This lake has a friendly face with its charming Gwondana-land forest and clear water. There's more space between the trees. The track is not overgrown. The well-kept ski huts signal safety.

*

The four o'clock sun is shining directly onto my face as it lowers itself towards the horizon.

Come evening, the Lake Dobson huts are filling up in readiness for the weekend. Six little boys are roaring around in the dark like a storm. One day they'll be grown-up too and this night will be a distant memory. Memory is the storyteller. I wonder if my nephews, who came here as little boys with my father, remember this place. Tomorrow I'll stop at Lake Fenton and the Lyrebird Nature Trail on my way back down the sixteen kilometre road to Russell Falls.

On the way out the next morning the road is bathed in brilliant sunshine. The rolling mist has completely gone to reveal the ridge line clean against an expanse of cerulean sky. And those afternoon showers? We're still waiting for rain.

The Mountain

The wind cuts cold through edge-sharpening sunshine,
blows holes in my brain, freezes thought.
Sleet sharp as glass splinters
keeps me pacing
between pinnacle boulders exposed.

Mist wafts across magnetic columns
roasted honey-brown by millennia.
Skinks scuttle from my heavy tread,
orange currant cluster and snowberry
greet the smell of dried gum-leaf underfoot.
A field of dolerite pimpled by moss
white, black and orange,
slants skyward,
its eucalypt crown sways and glistens.

The Mountain touched a longing I barely knew existed,
it felt like home.
I walk across its east-facing chest, upright, shoulders back.
Above, the voice of an ant-tiny climber
drifts down
to the nest of houses below.
The Zig Zag Track scales acute-angled,
a geometry of sun and shade.
A boy races danger down scree,
swift parrots dart red across the air waves.

Up top a breeze fans boulders jutting horizontal,
clouds veer sideways
beneath me, way down there
I see our ten acres
minute in the Mountain's lap
and the city stretched around the river flat.
A haze of ridges and valleys continue
westward, reaching for day's end.

A blueberry trail and the curl of pandanus
dress the path most travelled
from the Springs to Junction Cabin.
Sphinx Rock sandstone keeps watch
over bare tree tops still sprouting leaves after forty years
and the watery distance of hills and inlets.
Currawong cries hang in mid-air;
they sit in black bunches on grey branches,
huddles of gossip.

In winter snow brings squeals on a week day,
white-lined slender limbs,
a storybook snowman, a greeting-card forest;
in the muffled quiet, the birds cloit, cloit.

The mystery of the next bend beckons,
up and around, around and down
I stroll beneath plumb trunks,
to the creek gushing over the slip.
Along the lane from Neika to Silver Falls,
not far from a waiting car,
across shrubby Snake Plains,
you can feel expansive.

www.ingramcontent.com/pod-product-compliance
Lightning Source LLC
Chambersburg PA
CBHW062200100526
44589CB00014B/1889